The Book of Landings

Wesleyan Poetry

WESLEYAN UNIVERSITY PRESS   MIDDLETOWN, CONNECTICUT

Mark McMorris

THE BOOK OF LANDINGS

Wesleyan University Press

Middletown CT 06459

www.wesleyan.edu/wespress

© 2016 by Mark McMorris

All rights reserved

Manufactured in the United States of America

Designed by Quemadura

Typeset in Akzidenz Grotesk, Bembo, and Clarendon

National
Endowment
for the Arts
arts.gov

ART WORKS.

This project is supported in part by an award
from the National Endowment for the Arts.

Library of Congress Cataloging-in-Publication Data

Name: McMorris, Mark, author.

Title: The book of landings / Mark McMorris.

Description: Middletown, Connecticut : Wesleyan University Press, [2016] |
    Series: Wesleyan Poetry series

Identifiers: LCCN 2015035079| ISBN 9780819576330 (hardcover : acid-free paper) |
    ISBN 9780819576347 (ebook)

Classification: LCC PS3563.C3872 A6 2016 | DDC 811/.54—dc23

LC record available at http://lccn.loc.gov/2015035079

5 4 3 2 1

For Kim, as always.

Contents

Acknowledgments

Sections of this book were written while on fellowships provided by Lannan Foundation and the Graduate School of Georgetown University. I remain deeply grateful for their generous support.

Poems in the book previously appeared in *Hambone, Iowa Review, Critical Quarterly, Obsidian*, the Academy of American Poets Daily Series, PEN Poetry Series, and *Another Instance: Three Chapbooks*. "The Drums of Marrakech" first appeared in *Harper's* (March 2016).

The Fragility of Writing

Notes on a Trilogy

The Book of Landings consists of the second and third volumes of a trilogy. The first volume was published as *Entrepôt* in 2010. Around the time this volume was going to press, I started to think of lyric poetry as dubiously fragile and apt to crumble over time, to become vapor. The wordiness of the poem acted subversively, because the more words you have the further you are from the hard core of perception. But at the same time, confusedly, more words appear to lend weight to immaterial thoughts. To reach a state of durability, the poem needed fewer, not more, words. You needed words to act like stones, an indivisible geological unit. Or, you needed words to act like a mark made by the hand on the wall of a cave, like a physical cutting into a surface, such as a mark formed by cutting into a sheet of vellum with a sharp stylus. You needed a mark unifying the deformation of a surface—cutting into a block of wood—with its meaning. How to make a poem consist of such marks? What would such a poem be like? It would be brief, even fragmentary, for the operations of ordinary syntax would be minimized. Ideally, and also impossibly, such a poem would consist of one word, one mark only, a mark exactly equal to, and indistinguishable from, what it represented: a symbol. But obviously for the word to be durable it must be related to other words and to a sufficiently forceful perception of the world. A poem must consist of more than one word, and yet this plurality increases its fragility; but a word by itself is hardly anything at all.

Thoughts such as these led me to draw a grid of rectangles and to try to see by what relationships of "sight, sound, and intellection" the grid might be filled in with 12 words. I looked back at a page in Volume I of the trilogy from the poem "Gadji Beri Bimba," where hand-drawings are imposed over text. My reason for making those drawings in "Gadji Beri Bimba" had to do with a desire to efface the previously inscribed language on the page and to accentuate the presence of alien, non-verbal forms. But for Volume II, the impulse was not to efface but to transfix the word, to isolate it, to give it due respect, to heighten its word-ness, by placing it inside a rectangle. The geometry of the grids, and the graphic markings on the page, were what drew me at first, the permanence and materiality of marks as opposed to the immateriality of verbal meanings. The defacement of the two pages in Volume I left more to do.

I must have started by writing down a word in the square of a grid—a word like souk.

To write down any next word I tested several words in my mind against words previous selected, mainly for how they might coexist and throw up an imaginary field without encroaching semantically or phonemically too much on the terrain proposed thus far by the words already present in the grid. I paid no attention to choosing words that, together, could simulate the behavior of a lyric poem, or sum up to a narrative of sorts, because what I wanted to do was counteract the lyric poem's fragility. But there is a "logic" to the array of words inside any of the grids; the words belong together, and when read either horizontally, diagonally, or vertically, one word follows after another, but as a vector might bear away from a given trajectory.

The filling in happened intermittently, but the lexicon, or reservoir, was present right at the start. It came from the world engaged by Volume I and by the idea of an "entrepôt." In common usage, an entrepôt is a place set up for the trans-shipment of goods. Charting a multitude of separate in-bound vectors, objects enter the entrepôt from different external sites. The entrepôt collects these objects, formerly stationed or manufactured elsewhere, in one place —arranges a temporary meeting, as it were, of the disparate and the strange. But then, the objects are dispatched from the entrepôt onto new, outward-bound trajectories, towards their final destinations.

In my elaboration, an entrepôt is not a proper place, but a no-man's-land. Entrepôt exists apart from—on the outside of, or in between—places where national identity takes root and where nations have their durable geographical dwelling. Entrepôt punctuates the passage of bodies in space from one location to another. As such, the space of entrepôt is related to the refugee camp and to the ground bordered but not occupied by warring factions. The area around the port of a city is an entrepôt: polyglot, fertile ground for the emergence of hybrid tongues and argots. A slave ship is an especially violent entrepôt, a node in a network of other sites of gathering and dispersal: the dungeon, where slaves were temporarily housed on the West Coast of Africa; and the auction blocks of the Americas, whence they were scattered again to the plantations. These spaces—refugee camp, no-man's-land, seaport, ship, auction block, plantation—are abstracted from the geography of the nation-state. Dedicated to flux and transition, they frame the passage of bodies from nation to exile, but decline to offer the privileges of a stable society. For in the hiatus between previous origin and future destination there is a meeting of discrepant horizons. Gathered together briefly at the entrepôt is a heterogeneity of national costumes, which mingle and exert a reciprocal influence on one another, and which then emerge from the exit as hybrid or fragmentary forms. As a "no-place," entrepôt is related to paradise or utopia. But utopia, a vision of perfected polis, is the negative face of the system of transit, the inverse of entrepôt. Utopia is the destination longed for, but never attained, the form never concluded, in the passage.

In *Fragments from a Time before This*, the rectangles share a lexicon of entrepôt—that is to say, words dealing with exploration, conquest, warfare, migration, nomadism, transitional spaces like markets, sacred passages like thresholds and crossroads, voyages in time and space, together with words drawn from enterprises devoted to describing or facilitating movement, as, for example, the study of geography, cartography, navigation, even mathematics and cosmology. Because of this lexicon, the rectangles become vehicles for various specific metaphors: the grid of 12 rectangles serves to trap or arrest objects (words) in their flight; the grid reduces the chaos of forced migration, propelled by violent episodes such as wars, to the orderliness of a formal system, an abstract design; the grids clean up the situation, and impose stability on identities that are transient; the grids are formalized abstractions of various kinds of terrain, over which migrations take place. Hence, the borders of the grid are open to the border-spaces of the page, and open to the texts on other pages of the book. As the alphabet of the trilogy, words from the lexicon can "migrate" to other poems in both Volume II and III, evincing meanings from their usage in those contexts and suggesting another metaphor—another function—for the grids: origins, places to begin from, to go astray from.

Beginnings are repeated, then. The open structure of space in

"Fragments from a Time before This" became clearer to me at this point. In the first volume, entrepôt is a mediating term in a binary system of source and destination. The vector of passage looks like this: *here* $\longrightarrow$ *there*. But in *Fragments*, the vector of passage does not conclude at a destination. In keeping with the metaphor of the grids as places of departure, in this book space has the structure of a sequence of origins; or what amounts to the same thing, a sequence of destinations: *(t)here* $\longrightarrow$ *(t)here* $\longrightarrow$ *(t)here* $\longrightarrow$ *(t)here* $\longrightarrow$ *(t)here* $\longrightarrow$ *(t)here* $\longrightarrow$ . . . without end, the form of an infinite series. Entrepôt now expresses the mobility of a diaspora that has no limit: a metamorphosis of forms already hybridized, and a perpetual yielding towards otherness.

This perpetual yielding is made palpable by the fragmentary texts scattered on the pages of the book. This is especially conspicuous in the graphic layout of the sections entitled "12 Rectangles" and "Line Drawings." There one encounters inconclusive or distorted texts, together with brief meditations on the desert, on abstract painting, on nomadism; one encounters the parts of geometry, horizontal lines, vertical lines, spaces partitioned, words next to invisible borders. The scattering of pieces, even pieces of geometry, appeared to me as the product of a violent machine. And the ruined form of the pages brought to mind, not the detritus of the West, but that of scattered exiles in dissolution from what Empire had wrought, when the binary still held.

The explanation of the fragments was devised after the fact of the pages, upon the terrain of another metaphor. Overtly incomplete, the fragment of any object exhibits a dislocation in time from an original moment of assembly: what was once a whole has, over time, become *disiecta membra* (the "scattered limbs" of a body). As a synecdoche pointing to a greater whole, the fragment of an otherwise lost work is a broken piece, an intimation of more—a never-ending incitement to nostalgia. It is a memorial of violence done to, and suffered by, a body of work in its tradition from the writer's hand to the copyist or printer to the library, and down through time. Arrested in the present after a long and deleterious passage, the fragment, and the collage of fragments, both serve to mark the modernity of forms: all that we can today possess of the past are fragments from a whole that existed at some previous date.

In a serial poem, the fragment intensifies thought: "only by means of the sharpest focus on a single point can the individual idea gain a kind of wholeness," says Schlegel in the Lyceum Fragments. In my reading of "Fragments from a Time before This," the inscription of diaspora takes the form of the relocated fragment, the fragment of speech that has been displaced, sent out of its place and put out of its time, repeatedly. With the shift in the structure of space (here and there are identical), so that beyond entrepôt lies only another entrepôt, came a sense of limits—a boundary of which the first volume had no awareness. So long as I concentrated upon the basic structure of origin to destination, mediated by passage through an entrepôt, the future could still hold promise, which I had called Utopia in the first volume. But, now, with entrepôt generalized and equivalent to space, so that beyond entrepôt lies only another entrepôt, the promise of a destination was dissolved. The future retreated to the vanishing point of all perspectival trajectories. Entrepôt was shown to me in a new light, as the artifact of an epoch—the Age of Empire—prior to our own future, a future in which the structure of space had changed, in which transit led only to further transit.

For lots of reasons, this situation alarmed me. For one thing, it seemed as if in looking for an antidote to the fragility of writing I had instead found the opposite. What else is writing if not the future imagined? If metamorphosis is perpetual, what is the ground of poetry? Poetry needs the anchor of nations and the national language if it is to be read and kept in play, but a future in which the horizon is perpetually transcended will not have nations. This is a complicated thought, full of conflict, for me, since one of my impulses has always been to write against the grain of *national* culture.

But in starting again, I saw that so far as entrepôt is the space of migration, the space of the page on which fragmentary traces of peoples and words are made visible, then it is a space defined by multiple and repeated traversals. Thinking this I was led once more to Volume I and to the figure of the "palimpsest" from the poem "Auditions for Utopia." The surface of traversal—of migration as of writing—is like a palimpsest. It is never a blank page, but harbors in its pores the ink of previous marks. Volume III tries to get hold of this figure of the palimpsest. This book is conscious of actual physical geography and the limits to how far one can travel, to how much new space there is. Hence the idea of re-using surfaces. A city like Marrakech, like Barcelona, is built on top of previous versions of the city. These layers contain remnants or sacred relics or secular memorials or artifacts of previous lives, previous arrivals and departures, conquests, technologies, vocabulary, traces of earlier inscriptions, if you will. Both cities open onto the deserts of northern Africa, Barcelona by way of conquerors who came north out of Senegal and the Sahara to the river Ebro, and so opened a channel for cultural interaction, and Marrakech for reasons of physical location. But the desert, too, is finite, and the caravans traverse it only to turn around and go the other way, retracing, in reverse, their previous route and thereby overwriting the signs of previous passage. I like to think that those previous signs are the ground of what comes next.[1]

MAY 2015

Note

1. Some sections of these notes also appear in "Where This Thing Is Going," a statement on poetics for *The Force of What's Possible: Writers on Accessibility and the Avant Garde,* ed. Lily Hoang and Joshua Marie Wilkinson (New York: Nightboat Books, 2015).

Fragments from a Time before This

I.

12 RECTANGLES

SOUK	SEXTANT	CARREFOUR
EXILE	ACCRA	NOSTOS
TEMPLE	DUNGEON	VOYAGER
SCATTER	BIVOUAC	DAKAR

12 Rectangles

I was misled, and so landed here.
Many a tale is no different.
But now I must speed my leaving.
For proof I can offer a chisel
broken stone, water from a far-off lagoon
where the fish are blind. Will you deny
me this? Here is a fragment of what
I saw: the choice was mine, and not mine at all.
And yet I have no remorse.

wood splinters
iron ore strings

This is the tree of   rootlessness
I carry the pot and   the earth
and store the tree in   side my bag
One night the sky will   open
Stars bloom on the limbs   of caryatids
The Guinea tree and   guinep tree
united in a barren   adventure

nostalgic Gold Coast (   ) diaphragm
auction
                Absence of Earth

Somewhere along
the ridge of hue and cry
coaxing desire
while he travels

He has no past
no tense at all
—so to speak

While he stands at the front
door of the house, the house
will have chosen furlough
the house is disconnected

Stranded light
"prismatic subdivision of the idea"

(Mallarmé   )

I saw my love in a dungeon
Who gave me a sextant
I saw my love in a castle
Who gave me a slave ship
I saw my love on Main Street
Hand in hand with nostalgia
(Birth-cloud of bricolage)

Man-sized urns

disjecta

portico in shadow

Agora. Thinking that the thing is true for once
This worldly doubt become animate response
To unposed questions, gestures of a silhouette
We saw standing beside the great dam at Aswan
While beneath the flood the streets of another city
Wove their mysterious tales into the entablature
Of empires emptied of trackless wandering

cement mixer	Agora
janitor	golden walls
janitor	
	mosque
barman carrefour	
barren confessor	roaming

4 Rectangles

The long years are the sky
Lexicon lost | tongue
Who speaks to the temple wall
I heard shouts at auction
Who can ignore the hurricane
The oracle in the wood
Laughter on the barricades
Suitcases on railroad tracks

The long years are the sea

Somewhere there's a girl I swoon to translate
Haulers of steel
Marble fountains
Shore-marker
Shop-keeper
Ship-builder
Steam Gold Coast

The long years are the dust

From deserts fragrances come
Of letters without vowels, mouths
With cracked teeth to gnaw
Banana skins and logic
Trash-hauler
Tool-maker
Satellite-dispatch

---

is

Replenish   diminish

replenish(is)diminish   (of)

toolmaker( )souk   (as)

figure( )movement   ( )

bivouac	Accra

sea–wall

compass

slag–heap

dire

cross of pure sensibility

die-cast

Sought most desperately for of all the choices

Negative Pythagorean Curvature
mall( )metaphor( )mimesis

Convex swoon
Who roaming
Who Guinea
Who satellite

Shut beyond the confines of the world

Mandolin
dwarf palm tree
arak

Intimate songs in my ear
she whispered and used to sing them of a day

I saw my love in charcoal
Who gave me a bird of prey

Wilder-city in winter
Shrapnel emptily falling

LINE DRAWINGS

STAR–GLITTER	CARAVAN	WANDERING
MEMNON	LATITUDE	SIGNAL
SUNDER	PROSPECT	CONGO
LITTORAL	MERCATOR	PALIMPSEST

12 Rectangles

Lines on the Desert

In its rising the wind blows me towards you
where you are in the lattices

graph paper visible over the rocks
where I am in light mixed with powder

the blue is depthless solid
the land goes around the mountain

and continues out of sight
where I am is not an exact place

field theory says that a thing
has a pattern and a probable landing

you look for me in the particles
of noise streaming through the rectangle

under that mountain is a giant
asleep since the last thunderstorm

the clouds are his horses, abandoned
to latitudes the airplane divides and conquers

not where a flamingo stands in marsh grass
billowing white forms and the fuselage

The desert is a place without music
when you enter it you enter
a noiseless transparent stadium
of brown-green and ochre stubble
minimally raised into the wall
of ridges isolated under the clouds
to cross the plateau takes a day
of willful blindness
                              you have to want
what it has to set out close to sunrise
to leave behind the car park's tarmac
and rail-car platform and box-cars
and follow the writing of the terrain
to stand to touch a geological event

people who live under an open sky
ceiling of auditorium deep blue
and lilac hills at sundown, and the dove
clouds sprawling and changing volumes

by dictate of accidental and vacuous
whispers of desert winds calling
to copy forms marked down in folios
no scribe has inked, no illuminators—
what can they know of the uncharitable sea

the desert plane fosters geometrical designs
uncommonly OK with transience
the surface becomes twelve becomes one
with estuaries like open jaws

Once we found a route through the desert
we skirted the huge mountain

and on the other side discovered a city
the Romans had been there, the Vandals

other conquerors had abided or destroyed
en route to the sea, and left no building

the language spoke of them as a rumor
inside alien sounds heard by scholars

bellowed cheeks like a jazz trumpeter
to greet a newcomer, in the street of clocks

not caring ourselves to settle amid the troubles
the day found us in the street of going out

Roaming the streets of the city
on the street of drums

on the street of tanners
on the street of wheelwrights

on the street of a thousand rabbis
on the street of lanterns

on the street of fluttering birds
on the street of cobblers

on the street of a thousand muezzins
on the street of tailors

on the street of glass
where the fountain disports in sunlight

12 Rectangles

Line Drawing (blue)

—AFTER MIRÓ

A single line through blue
the blue over a canvas

it covers the entire window
myself on the other side

the surface has two depths
in neither am I awake

and speaking to someone like you
when we were holding hands

the canvas was our desire
pure ether for light's passage

the song went so deep inside
it was identical to bone

how deep the song went

the space lay in my garment
the space lay in and around

our hands that held the brush
inside a library of air, on a ship

following the line and singing
in empty space—

that drew the picture
I had of you in my mind

the line by itself, unrepeatable
ethereal song of landing

.   .   .   .

memories of the time
before archaic poetry

when we were still kissing
the wounds of our swords

and I sang dancing girls
on the threshing floor

from them the meters
were moths at twilight

brushing the flawed skin

Fulsome   like   Fuselage

Fulsome   (   )

                like
Fulsome   (   ) Fuselage

Line Drawing (white)

—AFTER MIRÓ

A single line through white
the likeness and the not-like

of a line that stumbles across
the country as seen from above

breathless land

cropless and borderless space

a line makes no sound
emptiness surrounding the line

cannot speak of things

or speak of the trace

What held his brush like a double

moved in a line (alpha)
visible in between

filling space with thought
(metaphor)

origin become alphabet
in line and vegetable things

citadel	sunlight
cliff-face	weather

digamma

BAMBOO	EMPTY	WINDED
MAUL	TYCHO	1914
SANTA	MARIA	CANIS NEBULA
EMPTY	SINISTER	ALEPH

12 Rectangles

Untitled Lines

Another day, another question
where is there an end of it
what is the line between
a drawing and a dithyramb
the way gravity grips mass
and an embrace, the horizon
and a limit you never cross
a rectangle without borders

Gravity bends a line of verse
where is there an end of it
just as it bends sunlight, bends
backs and promises to turn
and trace a blue line, on a sheet
that never concludes
liminal wandering back and forth
over the surface like thread

Brought to the land by forces
sent from the city roaming
over no-man's-land, between
nightfall and departure
border   nationless   trailing
where is the Maginot Line
that shelters the homecoming

The dogs are barking tonight
and you are awake to listen
only small noises are company
amidst alarms of somewhere
voices wandering back and forth
the waking and the sleeping
the dogmas and repetitive cry

sojourn disrupted by soldiers
exodus has always been in progress
by the rivers of Babylon, where
how can we sing King Alpha's song
where is there an end of it

Catalunya 1939
gasoline falls instead of rain
the night sky is red and thunder
of propellers shakes the brush
in a studio at Mont-roig del Camp
the artist's distorted bodies
that sprawl on fifty lithographs

the body's broken symmetry
unfolded like a paper cut-out

Where is there an end of it
to the ships hauling and divulging
ancestral births on new coasts
and new languages to the ceremony
when is there ever an end to it
souls blown like consonants
over an endless concrete esplanade

Where is there an end of it
is there never an end to it

Another day, another refugee family
the gathering and the departure

threading the aperture of mountains
(when is, where is there an end of it)

visible trails and movement—cacophony
—clay pots—cacophony of horses

another day, another archipelago
the blue fan-tail of a peacock

folded up and trailing feathers
over lawns of the Antilles, the fireflies

coming out at night, winking like words
a line traces a word in the dark

here ——————————————→ there

delve for utopia
where the gold is born

another day of the sky
unrelieved by contrails

Dug down to tubers
fingers curled about
alphabet bones of
clay pots and horses
cache of devices
clotted with beetles
singing underfoot
like shadows on grass
of birches darker
on a trail than pines
moving through a circle
of sun turning about
plasma folios printed
with starfish and starlight
cloudless temperate
washing earth's shores

land | water

water | land

bruised wind

Unfinished Lines

Consider the petals of an orchid
consider the appearance and disappearance
of weather and shadow, moisture
and morning sunlight in the making
of color, what the eye perceives
the hand draws to illustrate a mood
a wound or word, not that the flower
conceals the zero of Arab mathematics
or that between the abstract circle
and material plant the mind reaches
for stillness, the body revives a dance
of sound or seeing or nothing and thereupon.

It is then that a writer gets up and begins
to draw tentative lines to illustrate
the wind's cacophony, to master metamorphosis
that leaves nothing at the core of the flower
wherein there is only a where, a question
of relation, layers of a palimpsest, and interlinear

translation, such matters of uncertain luster
and as for us, there is only to decide
the surface for today's drawing, if it is to be
a cave wall lit by a torch or a lover's back
if it be an episode you care about at all
and a metaphor for things not in evidence.

If only there had been an instrument
to tell the flower from its replica
to say that this is the place, or the vessel
on high seas, the one you boarded
to say that this is the line you crossed
when I abandoned you to the fabulist
and went on by myself to the city of salt

from the side of everyone you loved
and might have been, in a time before this

And is it that then the voyage is a fable
The way we move over a wind-swept overpass
While the cicadas are singing in a bush
While where does it come from to circle
And join the morning clouds and the trek
That there would be an origin to carry forward
And that if it is tactile then to wrestle
News from a flock of birds and ancestors
Being that what else is the thing that defines
The going and forth, what else begins and falls
Only to begin, only to roam the sea-floor.

Ah, then it occurs to you to take up the book
At last, to add your sign (sing) to the folios
Hanging from clothes lines in the back-yard garden
So that when the tempo builds and the day
Decides to get going once again, you will have done your part.

THE BOOK OF LANDING

PAMPAS		URDU
SPEAR-CAST	GASOLINE	
TOPPLE		ANTIPHONAL
PERILOUS	CANIS NEBULA	THYME

12 Rectangles

Marginalia of the song
Triangle welded to octave
Decibels from steamers
Legend of the abstract city
A question of open form
Tracing dactyls of desire
Hand scoring the fable
Numbers drawn on sand

The horse latitudes bulging
elliptical curves
stitched onto the country

Sinew of the horse's neck
like marble, the flight of rock
gave weight to things of the air

gravity	Basra
tensor	gravitas

VERTIGO

12 Rectangles

The book of landing
earthen to touch
of pages left empty
creased like faces
the magi's treatise
an oasis delivery
delved by drought
falling heretical
in a grammar of games
infinite exchanges
Tycho saw in a glass
far-flung bivouac
of angles arabesques
spear-cast dialects
I heard them all
met with Santa Maria
and headless men

and then we came here
we drank sweet ale
aloft at whiles
amid the fullers
and we went thence
trailing tangled syntax
like tram-cars
like hybrid orchids
like mingling gasses
like every tong
and came thereafter
amid the droves
of the harvesters of cane
and then we went out
ancestorless amid
hereafter
and lay down our sign
amid the snakes
baking in the hot summer

and mayhap we built
a circle about a center
repeated bending
lines that storm flooded
and so misperceived
the route we bequeathed
and mayhap we built
a widening funnel
a light-cone of the probable
an empty hourglass
cross-banded at the waist
cave-dweller
winter solstice
and lay down then our temple
amid the beggars

and we came at whiles
like shirtless pages
seeking exact wording
wrinkle of low-born
genealogies set loose
amid the artisans
of languish and longing

and we went from there
and put sorrow behind
and came at whiles to this
whispering marketplace
and tethered the beasts
canis nebulae
amid the rough Bedouin

kites in a season of drifting
O where

ORCHID	ORBITAL TRACK	WAVE-FORM
AMPLITUDE	TENSOR	VALISE
HALT	DECIBEL	ZERO-DEGREE
LIMINAL	UR $\int_0^\infty$	BAR

12 Rectangles

BLUE-SHIFTED SPACE

FIELD THEORY

VOICES I heard as a child
O where have they gone
the whistle of tree-frogs and crickets
the song of owls at nightfall
O where are they now the call of

CONSTELLATIONS

blazing memories faded like embers
I long to encounter the ceremony
of wood-fires in a church-yard
O my heart why have you withered

children on the field as night comes
my time is gone by like an ice-cube
and the stars are dense as they were
watery memories I long to possess

water–carrier
metal-worker
slum-dweller

Looked at more closely in what light there was

weeds choking the number line
in other climates bearers of long famine

axiom

The small house and the water
wheel that spins the turbine
The river runs through a door
over the blades of the wheel
and trails down to a window

Into the culvert the swift water
passes like a feathery thesis
Trees filled with lemon blossoms
orchard once in a stone country

O where have they gone
the days that never existed

In a country of stone houses
the days that memory invents

II.

PIDGIN GEOMETRY

LANDING	MINERAL	SAUVAGE
EPISCOPAL	MARINER	INSIGNIUM
COLONY	ARCHIMEDES	DIRE
SAHEL	VICTORY	CACIQUE

12 Rectangles

Table of Unit Values

Twelve words on paper hung
from a ceiling, large sheets
the rectangles open to the sea

behind the words, amidst
the letters the flicker of a face
the land windswept and bare

each word is a sign-post, diachronic
particle trail to the labyrinth
of history in three dimensions

the grid is a simplified speech
not all words survived the voyage
to be present at our dialogue

and when I speak to you
the coming and going of the sea
water distilled from brine

these are the words I call on
these are the words I will use
to explain my circumstances

like soot on lamp glass
twelve words are the residue
of speech left from a blaze

LEGBA	INDIGO	CATARACT
CROSS ROAD	PLANTATION	DELVE
ANCHOR	LEIBNIZ	VENAL
MEGALITH	TEMPT	CONTIGUITY

12 Rectangles

On the horizon a cumulus of horses
Archimedes dead at Syracuse

There is only the presumption
Angled gesture at previous

There is no staying behind
To establish a cross road *Colonie*

Ledger of defeated marginalia
An audible geometry (speech)

And that the route is transient
Navigable sloping overland

Lexicon and lex identical
Fragments from a time before this

PICTOGRAM	COVE	TEMPLATE
GIRDLE	IMPEL	COLONY
WHIPPING POST	DIANOIA	STRANDED
HIATUS	CATHEDRAL	GUINEA GRASS

12 Rectangles

Whence cometh beauty, you ask
The dogged refugee, sea-weathered

Bearing the rabbit's white foot
One man with a crutch

Another with a boot of iron
Proof by approximate infinitesimals

Whence cometh the man with nothing
Whence the steamfitters

Another day brings intemperate weather
To wake beside a gully

To sleep and fall through glass
Who wrote screeds on property

What might song be if not number
Palpable and sun-lit caravan

This is how the sky always appears
Things have desire of their own

Appearances and disappearances
Clouds like a galloping horse

And palm trees are standing quietly
Latin insignium and log-book

Bound into fasces, and held aloft
To make a space open and replete

Wandering by a green cow pasture
Georg inventor orders of infinity

Word calling to other words, in transit
What you see creates the specimen

And so it is that the table holding
La lune sauvage is a hieroglyph

White roses are splashing color
Objects sending out lines of force

To diagram the physical weight of things
Gate posts like stone pillboxes

Oil lamp surrounded by bullrushes
Being an involuntary subject

And the garden of statues
Syntax by position organized as natural

In one place I saw the other place
Political designs defeated by their creatures

Heard tell of Panama, Honduras, Costa Rica, Cuba
By then the indigenes had departed

The night air around me was still
And I went mutilated then saying

City multiplied by city equal to city
To language the lang- gave birth

To language the land gave cacique
Oblique planes about to entangle

Whether the box-like interior was dark
Tower of surveillance ringed in by weather

"To tear wealth from the bowels"
Bought and sold molasses

System and axiom
Should your method be promising

Of the pidgin used in trade
Zeroed to hold a collective shape

What stultifies is majesty
Things that impel, steam power

Bought and sold iron
Prospect of Legba

And stood up the megalith
Built with labor from the barracks

ALGEBRA	CAST IRON	ECONOMY
FURLOUGH	DOUBLOON	METRICAL
TROUGH	BLAISE	GALLEON
PLINTH	MOLASSES	INFINITESIMAL

12 Rectangles

Some things happened as expected, given
The metropolis I lived in and the epoch

You could say that I followed an orthodox
Course and made the choices that were

Sanctioned within these limits I prospered
But there were other vectors in my life

I compare them to trans-celestial masses
Hidden from the most powerful telescopes

Invisible to normal methods of observation
Yet they cause perturbation in the paths

Taken by smaller bodies like the moons
Often I have looked at myself in wonder

And asked how I came to be in such a place
Amidst such alien gods and defeated men

From midnight to midnight, from landfall
To departure, time multiplied my encounters

With the sojourners of the earth, barbarians
Very like myself, until any camp I visited

Could have been where I was coming from
And any trading post could have been an origin

You need that coordinate to steer by
The distinction between homeland and hiatus

But that is the one that gets lost first
The infinite series of (t)here it always was

The lexicon would be small, invariably
No more than twelve words in circulation

I saw these were enough for their purposes
Mainly to tell tales of their voyages

And to negotiate things at the public market
Signals were improvised for private needs

It was tedious to learn these new tongues
But otherwise I could not have survived

There was no Common Speech, and we never
Stayed anywhere long enough to make one up

And so the tales were similar to one another
The pidgin limited what anyone could say

Regardless of what had happened to you
The particulars of it had to wait until

A suitable vocabulary was provided
Many signal episodes of my biography

Remained untold for long intervals
For then I could recall only scraps, a noun

Or a participle, a cuneiform wedge when what
I needed was a question, in order to begin

In this way only a small part of any lifetime
Reached the others, and even the person

Whose life it was soon lost the ability
To harbor its traces, for want of mimesis

EPOCH	TRANS-	WATER TABLE
PIDGIN	INVENTOR	GAO
TWELVE	BLAZE	GEORG
CANTOR	HORIZONTAL	CONTACT

12 Rectangles

	Scriptorium	Las Casas
	Ledger	Fortify
	Captain	Hawser
	Boiler	Darien
	Hospital	No–man's-land
	Ship of the desert	Man o' war
	Furnace	Pidgin
	Young shoots	Gun carriage
12 Rectangles	Molasses	Creole
	Rum	Bartolomé
	Landfall	Canon
	Raleigh	Log-book

III.

WHILE WE'RE WAITING

BARRACKS
short-term labor

sonne l'heure
whipping-post
steeple-jack
stone-cutter

bending backwards   forwards
bending backwards   forwards

bending backwards   forwards
bending backwards   forwards
bending backwards   forwards

Fragment on a Modern Condition

The beautiful dream of deathless
meadows stolen from the archives

The Orchid in Heaven

The travels come to an end
the world runs out of language

once, we learned to think of thought
and then to think of nothing

not as an absence but as a thing
a not-there like *Ceci n'est pas une pipe*

and invented the Holy Zero
to master the infinite number line

and then to think of ourselves
as thought's children, the makers

of questions and windows, consecrated
by logicians dressed up as seagulls

and in these thoughts we are correct
for a mind is like Penelope

a tool for counting and empty
weaving the seduction she unravels

encountering police at a checkpoint
everybody pretends to salute

the necessity of the state
the sun comes up again on the loom

As from vacuum particles arise
energetic in permeable space

so from our speech may it ever be
that a form enclose our spirit

whatever perfects the orchid
amidst the energetic stars

be perceptible and delay
in the meantime, while we're waiting

City of Palimpsests

I.

PLANTATION

Gun Carriage at Old Fort

In old forts, on the New World coast
one sees gun carriages left over
from colonial days. Their lips point to sea.
Below the battlements, the hill slopes
down to a paved road with trucks
and further out the white breakers rolling
cross-wise and cragged by the breeze.

What the sea writes is scraped and replaced
like the topmost surface of a palimpsest.
The thunder of cannon imitates the thunder
of waves breaking loudly on the coastline.
One writing begins another, moves inland
and withdraws, and in departure leaves absence
to be filled in again by a scribe's stylus.

The rhythm of the sea is the hand, blue-stained,
imagining a smooth landfall to imprint
with transitory illumination, the sunlight cast
over rose bushes and pink orchids, and onto
the rusty axels of the gun carriage—
light in which each detail of the wheel is alive—
until a cloud blurs the articulated shadows.

Anchored by the gun carriage, the old fort
once protected the frontiers of an *imperium*.
One language falters at the coast, another power
begins where land pulses out of the sea.
The palimpsest can have no durable speech.
Its anthem is no one's, a song of no man's land.
The space is delved by barbarian genealogies.

Out on the horizon, where the indigo sea curves
away from the sky that grows deeper steel
an oil tanker rides the great swells.
Closer to landfall, the window of tidal motion
through which the fort passes onto the page
opens and closes, like a lung breathing.
These old forts will survive the worst of storms.

The Great House in Various Light

The evening empty as a convex
coconut split down the seam:
not that it can be filled.

The evening empty as a gourd
that twists on an iron thread:
the rough skin of the sphere.

.   .   .   .   .

Not that there was a spoken word
to recall the moment of seeing
the short span when the clocks
ceased to revolve and hands
met in jest or benediction
time of the vortex into which
hibiscus and almond trees strayed
and windows made of aluminum.

The stars are suddenly remote
candescent petals night throws
above the yard, the beautiful things.

.   .   .   .   .

The great house is a hotel
and a museum of victory

how some lived at the epoch
of planters and governors

visible in the paintings
the armchairs and gilded glass

articulate artifacts
and floors polished by daylight

in a country of green hills
and water wheels and wagons

and sun coming out after a rain
the labor is hidden that built

the house long ago, and ploughed
the land to make it bear fruit

. . . . .

In British poetry, gentle woodland
creatures gaze at the hermit
with marble eyes lit from within.
A single bird defends the song.
Among the pines draped with snow
from the whole land only a secret
footfall teases the senses awake
like white breath on white canvas.

Ideal forms crowd the auditorium.
The sky deepens on the surface
of a lake, in a cradle of stars.
A coppice of isolated birch trees
climbs the mountainside to touch
the moon's scar, benevolent witness
washed of color and fragmentary
illuminating the village below.

.   .   .   .   .

In New World poetry, an invisible
river runs this way and that.
A car(t) eases on a bumpy track
over small hills and into shallows.
The world is a tangle of leaves.
Towards sundown a driver gets out
and pushes into the forest, drawn
by a noise he cannot identify:
perhaps the hiss of water below.
It's only the river on its way.

Ideal forms crowd the auditorium
things present and things past
scattered beneath the poinciana.
The car heads into higher country
then out into space where fields
suddenly lie down beneath the seer
cattle pastures and agricultural lands
that have always been there
watched over by the great house
from its hilltop, like a sentinel.

.   .   .   .   .

In British poetry, the forms
of desire darken with the change
of seasons: green leaves once
they fade and turn gold and fall
to earth, and make a carpet
in the forest, awaiting the rain.

For each season has its sonata.
Silence and sound in balance
belong to the decline of autumn.
In winter the notes are fewer.
Silence comes into its kingdom
crown of the father, who departs.

The world of white prepares
to conquer the earth with silence.

.   .   .   .   .

In British poetry, articulate hues
speak as they are visible to the mind
audible colors played on a piano
primary sounds in an empty forest.

And then above a lake, the moon
in motion suspended like a dancer
as the music temporarily ceases
depriving her body of its rhythm.

．　　　．　　　．　　　．　　　．

Ideal forms crowd the auditorium.
The light of day starts to fade
and a mist settles in the valleys.
The great house is lit from within.

.   .   .   .   .

As they were, in other windows
you want to see their ghosts
the slaves, like black posts
staggered through the fields.
You want to make a picture
that shows the strange overlords
at intervals watch the misery
of torsos laboring to plant
and harvest the seas of sugar.

.   .   .   .   .

The green beds of sugar cane
extend from here to the hills.

Bright heads grazed by the light
of paradise become its negative.

.   .   .   .   .

In time, would the land irritate us
as it must have irritated the masters
the tropical caress of the air unavoidable
getting up each day to see once more
the rolling green hills and cattle ponds
tranquil in the valleys, the horses
collected at the water trough, content
to stand or to walk over the grass.

A comely scene worthy of an oil painting
(fruit trees dappled with sunlight).

They have escaped from seasons
into the monotony of a terrible beauty.

(Who is speaking?)

.   .   .   .   .

Away from the coast
the car passes through
a shadowy green world
of tropical syntax
ragged slopes and curves.

．　　　．　　　．　　　．　　　．

What then was promised by the evening
lights that spangled about the hills?

.   .   .   .   .

Endless tall grasses, a landscape
composed of variations on a color.

The after-image of elliptical forms
transparent as the cry of a seagull.

．　　　．　　　．　　　．　　　．

A tablet of scripted exclamations:

there, a poinciana with pink blossoms
overhangs the road, there a scrawl
of fighting tendrils, an indigo grammar
of petals offering illumination
to fan-shaped pristine hieroglyphs
waving to greener punctuations
of banana trees and mango, a tangle
of writing over writing closed
to further interventions. Visible
palimpsest of a book without letters
the tangle of leaves has no secret key
and cannot be deciphered, wordless
monads travelling contours of silence.

. . . . .

Mimesis touches the world
with an imperceptible
tenderness, only hardly
like wind an Aeolian harp.

．　　　．　　　．　　　．　　　．

There is a point when the sky pivots
to face the dawn, to face the dark side
of personality, that of a sensible man
recanting the mysteries he embraced
as a youth, when the angels spoke to him
and he ran towards them with arms wide open
across a field, beneath the painted stars.

.   .   .   .   .

Say that the world is a drinking glass
containing things of the life and language
and say that a poet wakes up one morning
thinking of capturing for the future
those petals inside that glass, broken vowels.

A vase of orchids stands on a kitchen table.
Not that it is abstract, or a luminous
symbol, nonetheless it is an algebra
of forces, like the equations of space-time,
which rule outside the mental universe.

As if an image should leave its mirror behind
(the thing of which it is but a ghost)
like bodiless speech, and yet sensuous, in the way
a dream can leave its mark on the dreamer—
Esse est percipi, so speaketh the Law.

Wind begins to touch an Aeolian harp.
The great house is a place of articulation
word calls to other words, in transit.
Compelled by the beauty of flowers
the mind creates a space for other things.

.   .   .   .   .

(By British I mean Romantic idealist.)

Warm night descends
like a cloak. The whistle
of tree frogs supplies
a melody, and crickets
invisible to the moon
begin their Parliament.

The birds sleep with their young.
The air is otherwise still.

Birds as More Than Metaphor

Crusoe's was a land without metaphor
this sayeth the poet, and we listen
to cicadas stirring in the rose bush
and think that the voice of the earth
the waves rasping and billowing
to crash the sea-wall, and the noisy
sea gulls angling like foghorns in their flight
about the lighthouse, or on a rock—
that these instances of theatre demand
translation, not an auditor content
with solitude and a parasol, his palisades
staked to ward off a thousand cannibals—

certainly it is not enough to cherish
the oleander's dignity, but it is to speak
why we came and copied the mallard's
hieroglyph, traced the heron's flight
above the mangroves, and hewed a symbol
common to the egret and our melancholy—
and is it not then more than we can say
to say bird and mean what it is, the osprey
nesting on a post beside the reservoir
ornis   parajo   avis   oionos
and mean more than a tropical species
more than a silhouette, like a profile

blends with a girl who poses, undressed
on a verandah open to the salt breeze
that her figure coincides with the voice—
the myths have departed into mythology
and what is the form of desire to weld
the rain to our nerves, unless it be the form
displayed on sand, on the wind's writing
over the staggering mountains, were we hid
and formed a metaphor, to be our living.

Letters to Michael

Dear Michael (26)

Lines serve the painter and equally
the poet—because to draw is to write Paradise
in an auditorium, in the Book of Lists
late in the history of synaesthesia.

Artifact of Beginnings

Paradise must be a landscape inside
the language we inherit from the logos
borrowing from each person's childhood
to repeat the sounds of owls at night
the tactile image of mango trees evoked
by sunlight on a valley's hillside
where you stand, the color of earth
and there is a green table cloth spread
before your eyes for games of skill
rectangle edged in white, and mown grass
an artifact of beginnings and a song
to stir the classes in a way not repeated.

What is it that is about the idea except
everyone agrees there must be such a place
the comfort of mass delusion or a wish
that it is ahead and not over, and not a fable
written by old men with feverish hands
never mind their skill at the cithara
or their bondage in the land of the Egyptians.
Say then that the idea of it pre-dates
the Ziggurat of Ur, or the Olmec Heads
at Tres Zapotes. If only we had a metaphor
"ostrich plume ginger" as old as the idea
being the inventor of the design and a place.

Practical Green Table

I thought to write an elegy
as a reply to your questions
to pitch the word as far forward

like a dolphin out of the sea
over a threshold, to behold
the land as practical and green

as this table, a space to write
and walk into like a kitchen
hearing the conjunct vowels

what does a reader suppose
if not the promise of a text
the ultimate form at the end

of a chain of forms infinite
summed to a singular value
the elegy as a place to begin.

Worksong

In the mind are meters
written by sea-winds
a rough topography
bounded by emptiness
that the laborers sing out loud
here wi dig, here wi hoe
word of everlasting song

Paradise and Plantation

What else is Paradise besides a name Plantation
for things felt at the limits of the mind
the stirring in shadows underneath a willow
of white flowers nestled in spears of grass
harbor of tired laborers going home, their forms
like waders in high boots, the sea drawing nearby
and in stepping across a rigid rigorous field
abruptly the mountains rise and gather them in
they regard the valleys and think nothing
cancels the voyage over the ground they hoe
save that in the distance where sky meets orchid
and stolen language bleeds into the clouds
a place begins to be formed out of the body's fall.

Untitled One

There is a pictogram based on a river
that empties into a cove, where ships gather.
The scene forms a template for painting
of things that girdle the body
of the earth and impel sea captains
to try their luck setting up a colony.
In time a whipping-post appears
the torch of progress gutters.
Though stranded without wit, the sailors
refuse to call hiatus to their labor
of building the cathedral for worship.
The long guinea grass watches them at work.

Untitled Two

The one named Legba they didn't forget
in crossing the blue waters to the New World.
Fear was like a cataract in their heads.
They planted him at the cross-roads for luck
but day by day the plantation prospered
with tough men to delve trenches for sugar
anchor of the economy. The same epoch
which saw Newton, Leibniz, and Marvell
produced the venal calculus, wherein the gods—
their megaliths toppled and crumbled—
were held in abashed contempt. Pirates and
prostitutes in contiguity defined my house.

And this shall seldom chance

When she comes back the day is still drawing
to twilight, and the wind is fresh. The
clouds move hardly at all in the windows.
The feeling you have is of questions
beginning to nose forward like feet in wet grass
and the pace is slow, rhythmic, pastoral.
There's no reason to spin up the siren
alarms are common and leave things as they were
mute or pregnant, and bathed in half-light.
It is always there, under the surface,
voluptuous chords half-sensed, a whisper
(trailing fingers across a bowl of clear water)
that once you felt could rise up and demand
obedience from the most nonchalant pedestrian—
that man in a black suit waiting to transit
the boulevard, while mules and ox carts
lumber slowly into the future of perspective
into birches, into moonlight, and finally vanish.
Today is another matter, with rain dripping
from the gutter after a week of snowfall.
The chords are shining in the distance, like elms
lining a field you want to lie down in
and her beside you, oh yes, for a change.
The sound they make is tentative
but audible, the sharp notes well-spaced, shapely

with room to breathe in and together
and time suspended in the gap light crosses
from thing to thing and thing, the thing
you look for in the brilliant decline
of afternoon over the back-yard rose bushes.

Past the torn fence where trash cans scatter
the whisper gathers force and starts to invade
a space you thought fortified against surprise
such dithyrambs as keep a body awake at night
parting the curtains to see what the dogs
already know of shadows in the alleyway.
Another daytime drama peters out in the envelope
of twilight, which turns chill towards dawn.
Disappointed—not really, not by that name at least
since tomorrow a voice might send metaphors
of itself over the transistor radio
breathless and new with common purpose
like the unforeseen discovery of the lunar orbit
or the origin of starlight, replaying
as certainty what was promised, at other times.

[Letters to Michael: Dear Michael (18)]

Letters to Michael

Dear Michael (21)

What is the cause of faith
in mimesis if not the way
it enacts the world again?

II.

MARRAKECH

The Drums of Marrakech

1. *(History)*

From Senegal to Barcelona
the distance is that of a polity
an empire founded by Sanhaja
Almoravids of hostile love
nomads who broke musical
devices and put a stop to dancing
who before the New World
faltered under the Papal cross
divested things of this world
of the sounds and imaginings
pledged to make the mountains
a home for men soon to perish.
The empire stopped at the river
Ebro and the horses turned back
to seek Madrid and Valencia
on routes laid down to weld
the continents and conquests.

In time *Los Reyes Católicos* broke
the fellowship of scholars
in Andalucia, the lyric
and Hebrew and Arabic poets

passed to exile in the south
to places like Tamnougalt
annus mirabilis
1492
Año de Reconquista
the conquest of America begins.

These matters I knew about
entering the circle of drumming
hearing the prayerful chants
like Rastafari in exile
in Marrakech the old medina
built in the eleventh century
demolished in the twelfth
from which the Sanhaja rode.

2. (Kingston)

Perchance I had the occasion
to interview an old dray man

one day in downtown Kingston
to press him about his notions

where did he think he was
where did he think the sounds

arose from that he heard
in his mouth and the streets

in the bars and rum bottles
and Toots rattling the jukebox

and he said out of the earth
and he gave me a huge grin

and kissed his teeth and took
off for the department stores

and so I went back to reading
stories about Atlantic migrations

of bottom-of-the-barrel men
from England and the fables

they planted as extra crops
in the sweet-potato gardens

of the old plantocracy
and no one lives there today

3. (Metaphor)

Whatever else disappears
the feeling of a sound

secretly or openly like a vowel
survives the ocean

the floating dungeons
imitate the caravans

the auction blocks
the negative image

of altar and pulpit
limned in cathedral light

copying the rhythms
of sea-borne movement

a hand extends to hand
over blue-shifted space

through the language
we construct audible

surroundings like a market
where things come and go

4. (Marrakech)

Every night, night after night
in pockets across the esplanade

of the Marrakech medina
they set up a ring of benches

fetch out the darboka and def
and string the gundbri's lament

the music is unstoppable
in the circles of light the old

women and their daughters dance
a stately movement of the feet

hearing in those sounds something
of what I imagined the night

under stars resembled to people
wandering between two cities

you become like the featureless air
you lose track of your beginnings

5. (M'hamid)

The drums across the esplanade
were still loud in my memory, when

I stepped out of the bivouac's arch
to smoke yet another cigarette

the twilight had not yet appeared
soundless empty land

torch-light spread out in three
dimensions to inflate the skin

of the visible in which I stood
sounds waited over the dunes

all the while from the beginning
over hard-packed sahel

along the limb of a triangle
the caravans were in passage

the camels kneeling and walking
like dunes or breathing or the sea

their riders hardly urging
forms darker than the darkness

through which the sky pours
fragments of visible desire

whatever of actors and their voices
the desert consumes and erases

the air keeps a catalogue I thought
signs that stir in the mind

of travellers partial to mimesis
the night air around me was still

the voice of the mobile drums
entered the Valley of the Draâ

people stood around to listen
the drums pushed their signals ahead

of the caravans bound for Zagora
on the vertical plane the empty

space was perforated by history
some of the stars were visible

perfectly aligned like nuggets
of white gold in a lake of tar

the drums were an echo in air
of savors from an entrepôt

carried upon the wind's pages
the future had left no marks

6. *(Essaouira)*

In the cold sea on the west
coast of northern Africa
I looked for the profile
of the continent to which
the slave ships went long ago.

Where we can live
Live a good good life
And be free.

Nothing except the sea
was ahead when I looked
as if there never had been
a land to get to to land on
only the edge of vision
to fall down and not even
an underground railroad
to light out for the free.
In the negative Paradise
men had to improvise
wearing crocus-bag pants
marooned in the hills.

The sea had no knowledge
of these matters occurring
but still I drew a hand-
full of it on my forehead
out of respect for drums
I heard in the Marrakech medina
the rhythms I imagined
went abroad in the ships
moving there and doubling
over the sea's unruly pages
across the hard-packed sahel

Agadez to Zagora—
the caravan's archipelago
lamped by constellations
native to the south
(the desert's Croix du Sud)
on a three-month angle
there and looping around.

The sea moves and doesn't move.
Salt water evaporates.
Eventually the sun dries
the forehead and the skin
holds no print of transit
like the sand you disturb
the road is forever missing.

7. (Tamnougalt)

In the ksour of Tamnougalt
a road branches to the Jewish
quarter, the other road bends
to Muslim houses and the mosque.
Much of the town is hidden.
The streets bore through tunnels
built to regulate the weather.
The air smells of dried mud.
The ksour is a habitable labyrinth
fortified by tamarisk wood
lit by the occasional air-shaft.
Partitions are plentiful.
Any road leads to a carrefour
tongues meeting at a permeable
triangle inside the labyrinth.

Wandering like a translator
you see people kept hidden
from orchard-light in the palmerie
where the air is not as cool
learning underground paths
learning exits and entrances

inside the regional market
reading by lamp the book
from Jerusalem and writing
pages into it of their passage
along the scrawling river
going back to a time of legend.

No matter the curse of setting forth
in transit through alien spaces
you carry the origin with you
to the destination and abode
you once saw rising from the bleary
surface like a mirage, a city
in form perverted by the forces
of countless unconnected things.

8. (History)

The multitudes mingled
in the train of armies

from Senegal to Marrakech
from Sevilla to Cordoba

Andalucian kingdoms
drums were forbidden

the empire was temporary
dynasties rose and fell

in mimicry of the sea
which forgives no hubris

darboka and def
dominate the medina

in time for my arrival
and today I heard the drums

performances of the voyage
like a thing past remembering

9. (Method)

To read an alien sky begin
by learning the imitative
clouds above the battlements
cradling the cannon
they compose an alphabet
for exiles and a history
and their tongues are folded
over into scrolls that open
at night and beckon new stars
from their invisible houses
to festoon another departure.

Letters to Michael

Dear Michael (22)

I visited the last city
from which I send to you poems
in the form of starlings
released at first light to animate
the featureless heaven.
Know when you read it it was
my hand that held the pen
that spilled the symbols
I had then in my mind
in copying from the Book
of Nihil the gist of things
let loose in the open air
the particulars of a city's
design. On the last evening
in the street of jongleurs
I thought to have enough
detail to write a postcard
to you on love's lost labor.
The print of hooves filled with water
I am familiar with like I know
my own mind, which is to confess
hardly, nonetheless I send
word of them to your keeping.
Think of me and be well.

Dear Michael (23)

If you write a book which no one reads
does the book autumnally fall in the forest?
Time was when the scholiasts amused
their courtesans with words of the furthest
most sensitive ether, between the *fons communis*
and its redactors interposing variants
on which sign and sing changed places
down the illuminated centuries. A city
is not a folio that survives to dominate
the future of ideas, or that musters out
with remnants of the imperial cavalry
being the palimpsest of Archimedes
all things to all men, the site of effort
and negation, whence leaves of the mind
tumble in and tumble out like quarks.
Below the surface is only another surface
the most reckless sentence of them all
and yet how can you say it is not material
to the good life, to know where and when
the error first appeared, in the trusted hand.
Awaiting your counsel I am etc. as always.

Records

. . . . .

Before the astronomer's table
a circle with a demon inside
demons with wings of a bat
(Before the astronomer's table)
overhead like an armada of ships

. . . . .

Time of the weed, time of bramble
along the bank of a canal
muddy with old newspaper
close-held surface to write on
to dance as with desire
black letters where roads meet

. . . . .

Tonight in the city, only the chains
make soft noises like bells
only the dogs are awake
the fences lean over
to scrape their elbows
on stone and broken glass

III.

BARCELONA

Barcelona Series

Everything you see in my pictures exists. —JOAN MIRÓ

In 1939, while living and working at his family's property in Mont-roig del Camp, Catalunya, Joan Miró composed a set of lithographs in response to the civil war. Barcelona had been bombed the previous year by Italian and German planes, killing more than 1,000 people. After a month of fighting, the city fell to the Nationalists in January. Valencia and Madrid fell in March. Once in power, Franco's regime murdered an estimated 10,000 to 28,000 citizens with presumed ties to the Republicans. Form in art follows from crisis.

The motifs of the city are not visibly present in the lithographs. The eyes found on every page—many eyes drawn in a single head, three eyes placed vertically on an arm—suggest the labyrinth of alarm or surveillance through which the mind passes on its way to recoil. What you see is a reflection of seeing—a looking at looking back, a blindness. The drawings pay homage to things that are not there.

(Lithographs)

What he sees when he thinks about the city from his studio cannot be put in an image the line is what he sees two legs two arms raised up the head reaching down to touch the back

The head has three eyes a large star in black the nose has teeth upside down above a jaw that is a stomach walking the bomb or spider

And somewhere on the page the marks of the night sky with stars close to the arms tracing now the body is empty glass porous to space the space behind the space and gigantic

In an open mouth is a mouth with teeth pointed and oval eyes an eye beside a vagina an eye in the neck an angel gliding he sees inside his head negative sun when thinking of the city forms a bestiary

This is happening somewhere else in his head beside the beautiful buildings the two arms flung up through the face like an upturned frying pan the heads of the two lovers upside down looking and joined to a heart-shaped abdomen to a piece of wire this dancer has knobs for feet like the spider this one a wedge of iron does she sink does she float nobody has a ground there is space and things in it he thinks I must put down what space looks like when there is no boulevard

No accurate mirror for the multiplying limbs and eyes not knowing what to think not looking looking is this a troupe of school children is this a posture of wailing signified by the angle of the head the arms lifting

And if you reduce the organism to a line a dress on a coat-hanger let me strip her to see what if the abstract dwindles and her head like a spiral bull's-eye sits above a vagina where the nose of a profile and three lips and an eye hermaphrodite genitalia

When he thinks of the city he sees an aeroplane like a bird-fish and a planet bowling ball the neck flares into the mouth of a trumpet the neck tangled no air can pass get out and instead of screaming there is geometry

The ribbon tails overlaps itself spills into smeared along everyone turns about the black mark of lines wearing a dress or a triangle the parade of wire looks like looks out looks back standing on nothing this gentleman is a bird tied to a woman's body in the shape and feet

What he sees when he thinks about the city is a jaw with factory towers the body is made of space the right arm has four eyes and a long neck holds a head out like a hairbrush

One man fills the rectangle he is flat equal to the surface the torso and arms are a single line making the shape legs stuck into the shape and disks where you expect the feet there are bent tubes

Two arms have two eyes fingers are lollipops and curling hairs two necks have heads one body and a neck without a head the moon is a boomerang here jammed into the side of someone floats upside down there is no gravity

A catalogue of elements: moon, star, genitalia, neck, wire torso, triangle, hack-saw blade, two marbles, fingerless, bent tubes, diamond, mouth

What he sees he thinks the paper shows a block of wood with a face carved into it jagged mountain range cartoon inside the upper jaw head down and above the ankles a wedge hung

The chest has star cluster dust vulture blots the visible span parade of wire creatures biomorphic strings disjointed or blocked forms and thrown up the city's population an old man and a chicken and a face attached to an eel's body wiggles

Calligraphy of walking giant thumb-smear form follows

The swift perception of new things here is a dancer this is a bull's front this is a harlequin's costume in black and white this is an angel's wing this is a neck it feels like disorder when he thinks about the city in space bent and folded

The initial pattern defeated and thinned distorted from what he thinks the surface glass of space with stars and breasts a heavy cannonball stars and breasts destroys the way in

Nose like a spigot walking I see a human diver with her legs up eyes set in pockets of dust and a little girl the ribbon unravels shape on shape and

A bag of sand weighted to fall curving leg stands on a neck the other leg cocked over a blot sphere the being lacks definition star like a paper cut-out

The belly and thighs over there across the lintel an alligator with hack-saw on his back guards the surface sideways upwards which the nipple the heart or testicles smoky windstorm tries to eat the balloon

Chin taken aback horseshoe flying hair or wings fixed to a bent triangle her chest what things you think liquefied floating to the stars two figures elongated free from mass like wearing a nightgown

What it would be like if everything falls together accident substance jumbled together what is gigantic is near what is small is tied to a string tied to the fan crosses into a point where lines meet up the point of a hand almost touches the star

Filling up space are things or forms no mirror divulges to the painter looking over his shoulder like a coquette and forms collapse become reduced to curve shape bounded or looping wires one string to a figure like a numeral on a cave wall

Hapless loaf is this what they seem to him the people thinking of the city he goes back to when the stars come out over Mont-roig del Camp he can spot the bloated jaw of factory tower teeth razor wire where the face splits in two

What he tries to do is find the way a line moves across the page to say what is in the painter's head like a writer once put down a form to say he was here and went but made it simple this is a lung this an angel's wing things in his mind day after day things in every corner when you look up you see things like a fist, like a face

Mouth in passage from what he thinks to what he sees on the paper something interrupts and changes the trace of parts stuck on

A ladder an eggshell with a key and three spider legs everything big and tiny in the one space the page is not like seeing a city it feels like

If he could eat the star if he could float from the orange what can the moon avail its points can damage the heart some kind of animal

If he goes to the city is this what he sees instead of buildings the citizens like pipes twisting wire the forms just barely of a person

One triangle in black one triangle in white together they make the skirt for a dancer her neck is a piece of string her head an ink-blot sphere of trapped light

To write the approximate form for the thing in his mind by looking at things near about the long pipe bodies of the king and queen together as a single object in wood, in smelted bronze comes to the studio to alter the idea and a hand works to spell the constellation of bird and face and labyrinth and star

(Things he omits today)

Today he omits the things he saw instead he puts in the things he sees when he remembers the city he lived in once to put in place and manifest the thing it looks like in his head when he thinks and when he reads the news of the city in the last evening of its anarchy and liberty like speech the dancers and poems from the fifteenth century and the names of streets

Today he omits the farm and rural mountains the snail as big as a dog in the foreground and the strip of ploughed ribbon from the surface but puts a star in and dancers bend their backs the country the city the boulevard the lake the Catalan peasant smoking a pipe these he omits from the things he traces

Today he omits the electrical machine powering the sodium lamps at Universitat all across the surface there are no machines steam compressors motor cars ironworks textile mills devouring organic spontaneity

Today he omits barricades and Valencia and the columns of soldiers on parade in all of the surface there is no balcony to what he sees he thinks is taking place in the city under smoke

Today he omits he is blind to the city at empty Plaça Reial the market and galleries and what happens in his head is what he thinks when he reaches for ink and a page to draw things that oppress the mind the collapse of space the distinction of parts lost to the bestiary the city has become in his lifetime

Today he omits women carrying roses the whistle of artillery projectiles El Dia de la Rosa arcing over the Ebro there was a time I did not witness and there is a time I will not witness he says to the drawing lying on which he sees

Today he omits Lenin Barracks column of militia Italian anarchist he omits Catalunya Lliure in the Mont Juic prison they never knew whether they were in prison or awaiting execution the executioner did not have the answer chance maybe or a new thought on a day when it was day

Today he omits some things he might have put in when he thinks of the city he sees in his studio at Mont-roig del Camp beside the beautiful buildings he forgets to omit the fact of tenuous string

Barcelona 1939

sunlit plaça
sgraffito
street car
solo performer
cop

marble fountain
tongue
statue
delivery truck
mill

pedestrian
bicycle
topcoat
street lamp
tree

pastry and bread shop
handcart
festes
mailbox
prostitute

waiter
wagon
umbrella
circle
green bird

Things

(Baroque Modernisme)

The eye is an elementary shape
like a stone it sits in a canal

cut into a stick that is flat
and because it rests on water

in a bowl like a compass needle
an eye borrows the light

like white stone carved to the semblance
of massed workers and heroes

what if when you looked at a surface
you saw eyes looking what if you were

expecting a tailor's guild hat
and heard only the sounds of wire

(Theory of Previous Value)

On the boulevard friends
and enemies take cover

blood of roses and swords
imprinted on their eyelids

heard clapping the grey city
the 10,000 organ pipes

and free-standing looms
of industrial revolution

the motorcycle engines
today is another rumor

of Vandals and the silos
beheaded under the gallop

(Preparation)

At the limit missing the absence
of manufactured things

constant helicopter blades
unnerve the land-fill coast

on the other side Cyprus
on this side my grandfather

at Mont Juic citadel of the city
light through the iron bars

invisible does not fall across
his face with its pockets

what he sees when he thinks
about the city is a drawing

(Anarchists at Jaume)

In the place of the city a desert
que la cultura no pagui l'estafa

animals live inside the wind
not the same as missing

so that the overweight cabinets
of unclaimed property values

and hyphenated water to say
nothing of the better angels

in that time aware of peril
mas cabro retallat els colons

stood guard three nights
at Poliorama rooftop copulas

(Final Payment)

The man with a bulldog in his face
kneels down to receive the benediction

he expects that this primal blessing
will cancel the emergency actions

that of the errors soon to be
precisely catalogued a few will escape

that the intent was noble, the method
necessary, and the result propitious

are settled questions to the benefit
of posterity and neighbors, however

much others may yet contaminate the record
the sleep of the just is his anchor

(Stranger Washing)

Across the courtyard on a balcony
that is not quite in the sky

a woman hangs out the laundry
she is not my woman, Barcelona

of the laundry she hangs
the white sheet is not a flag

the red is not a political idea
she thinks that the overcast sky

conceals more than the sun
behind the grey tarpaulin crouch

the stanzas that bring unrest
(the rain inside her chest)

small favors promised by the clock
have refused to comply

she belongs to the stone-work
seraphim at the Palau de la Musica

(Untitled)

When you arrive in Barcelona
the war will be over. The victors
will have staged their parades
on Passeig de Sant Joan, the cursed
will have fled, swelling the camp
of refugees inside the French border.

When you arrive in Barcelona
the dictator will be dead, who made
the war that won't disappear.
The languages have come out that went
into hiding after the victory.
The sky of Barcelona is the same sky.

When you arrive in Barcelona
the interval of the war is a legend
voiced in books by old men speaking
finally. Every city has its secrets
inaudible to the augur. Where
the bodies are buried is still buried.

When you arrive in Barcelona
the thinking of a painter is a doing
by hand what a writer does abstractly
or not at all with the language
of words whether in Catalan or in
the tongue of things everywhere visible.

When you arrive in Barcelona
the war will exist only in the mind
on paper as language in the poems
of expatriates and the histories.
Miró didn't put war into his lithographs
made during the worst of the war.

(Untitled)

You arrived in Barcelona to see what the city had left of the war
the Civil War from the previous century which the poets wrote
and you read elegies about to mark the coming of terror to Western
Europe before the real war started everywhere you thought to see
whether a city could keep its history in the air you transit to the
bronze statues and the buildings still standing like the Telephone
Exchange building at Plaça Catalunya, 16, whether in the smelted
grillwork and stone fountain at Espanya one might not still as-
certain by means of seeing the things that terrorized Miró in his
farmhouse at Mont-roig del Camp thinking that it should not be
possible for the life of the epoch to be as if it had never endured
mutilation except for what the books say and the children of the
children of the dead in their lost graves said of things handed down
in the prohibited tongue over the interminable years when the
dictator was not yet dead Miró had passed away and Tapies and
remnants of the International Brigades had come and gone back
home and no one could find Lorca's bones how can everyone not
be remembering the war all the time they are sitting in the Metro
stations watching video of their gorgeous ancient city dating to
the Roman empire the war you thought must always be everywhere
in the wet clothes hung below the window flower-boxes in the
baroque entablatures in the cathedral vaults in the art nouveau

mansions in the socialist clubhouses and anarchist bookshops in Raval but the war isn't like it is in Belfast with gigantic murals and the wall separating factions the war is not available to outsiders they have their own wars to forget in Barcelona like wars anywhere you want to forget you keep moving the desire to write or draw has no choice but to betray the speech it wants to serve the speech which is already over the writing which mimics grass trampled by hooves in a long punishing interlude from entrepôt to entrepôt in a time before the city was falling and getting farther away from things in his head seeing the city in a time before the soldiers arrived

Near to Mont-roig del Camp a Roman aqueduct brings water for the strawberries in the water there is writing to see and decipher of the transit of coat-hangers and scarred winds blowing through in-dividuals thin as bathroom tissue thinner than smoke and wire in the Pyrenees closer to the city than Andalucia where laborers are hunting rabbits to eat the language survives outside the physical space marked by traces of his thought by the time you arrive in the city

IV.

LAST LETTERS

Letters to Michael

Dear Michael (24)

Twilight in the city
of palimpsests, and hiatus
of signals once expected
to consecrate the poem
the power of a church
the power to make martyrs
of unfortunate children
though I have heard tell
of their arrival from lands
once promising, in books
not prone to superstition.
Their tale begins and ends
where we begin and end
on a journey to celestial
coordinates, over scrappy
terrain in the after-wash
of hooves, over the greenest
landscape short of heaven
your heart could covet
the chants of gather-me-home
the rhythms your limbo limbs
remember from cities of mud.

One day I'll read the poetry
of Zanzotto to remember.
One day I'll tell the difference
between wound and chalice
relic of blue-shifted space.
In the meantime as it was
your thought is my library.

Dear Michael (25)

If poetry is not bread
to fortify the righteous
is it because we miss
in it the savor of contest
the whisper of blessing
over a martyr's name
the light of sacral plans
to take the citadel once
and for all, or give it up?
On the original streets
lit by the sun of nineteenth-
century novels the workers
are gathering to march
for their dignity and bread.
The planters did not die
of happiness. Other exhibits
show their meadows
their horses and women
the English sunset in lands
never more than a sigh
like a vowel far from home.
We ask too much when of
the little that we have.
In good health fondly yours.

The Last City

There is always another city
you come to Rissani
the people, their tongue, their way
of navigating the streets, their gods
you say that this is the limit
of cities beyond which is neither
east nor west but only the curve
of earth falling into the valley
pastured by the sun and walked
by stars of an abstruse geometry
there is no further to go than this
you are at the frontier
where all roads and all rivers
sink into the sky like a prayer
only the exile whispers
as he stares deep into a calyx
there is always another city
there is a city called Sijilmasa
that was forgotten by the diggers
of labyrinths and archangels
city of concubines harsh city of slaves
gold and spices city of weeping
city of boulevards and gardens
ibises and fountains and the wind
culling an alphabet from a bird's walk

there is always another city
hidden in your footsteps like a song
sung by a harlequin singer
as the poplars tremble and the wind stirs
there is always another city
say if I travel past this milepost
the road will become its double
the journey home will lead me to you
woman who bears her soldier
to the twilight of cathedrals
the city strikes twelve in her face
there is always another city
another Acropolis another citrus grove
to replace the one you long for
there is always another city
and in her palm you see the zero
of an orchid plucked from a guitar
there is always another city
hidden in your belt, the city
of empty libraries and tambourines
the city you call the last
city, the city of iron, the ordeal
and quest assigned to those who eat offal
a city where there is no language
to name it except the tongue of lizards
there is a city never visited
by Herodotus which is stranger than this
not even a book, only the idea of a book
the thought of Paradise, the idea of a reader
and a place to set it down

ABOUT THE AUTHOR

Mark McMorris's recent poetry collections include *Entrepôt* (Coffee House Press, 2010), *The Café at Light* (Roof Books, 2004), *The Blaze of the Poui* (University of Georgia Press, 2003), *The Black Reeds* (University of Georgia Press, 1997), and *Moth-Wings* (Burning Deck, 1996). He is a two-time winner of the Contemporary Poetry Series Prize, and has received The Gertrude Stein Award in Innovative American Poetry. Born in Kingston, Jamaica, in 1960, he has taught at Brown University, the University of California at Berkeley, and Georgetown University, where he is currently Associate Professor of English. A critic and fiction writer as well as a poet, his work has appeared widely in periodicals and anthologies in the United States.

A reader's companion is available at markmcmorris.site.wesleyan.edu.